Do Elephants Talk?

PATHFINDER EDITION

By Peter Winkler

CONTENTS

Thirsty and hot, 12 elephants plod across the fried African landscape. The water hole is less than a mile away now, and everyone in the **herd** is looking forward to a good, long drink. Tired **calves** want to stop, but mothers and aunts nudge them along. The older animals make soft, soothing noises. "We're almost there," they seem to say. "Just keep walking."

Suddenly everyone stops. Huge ears stretch out like satellite dishes. After a minute or two of what seems like silence, the animals turn and walk away from the water hole—fast. As they go, the adults huddle close to the calves.

So what happened? Why did the elephants change their course? They seemed to be listening to something. Whatever it was, they got the message to flee! Yet human ears heard nothing.

Elephants make plenty of sounds that humans can hear, such as barks, snorts, roars, and trumpet-like calls. Often a herd will use those sounds to talk with other elephants. But they weren't in the air this time.

SECOND LANGUAGE

For years, elephants puzzled observers with this type of behavior. But now scientists have solved the mystery. They discovered that elephants have a "secret" language for communicating over long distances. This special talk is based on **infrasound**, sounds so low in **pitch** that humans can't hear them. The sounds can travel several miles, allowing the six-ton animals to keep in touch across grasslands and forests in Africa or Asia.

To study elephant infrasound, researchers use special equipment that can record low-pitch sound waves. Another machine, called a **spectrograph**, translates the recorded sound waves into images, or markings, that we can see. The images stand for various messages.

▶ **Family Gathering.**
When danger lurks, adults huddle close to protect their calves.

▲ **Real Nose-y.**
With 50,000 muscles, an elephant's trunk works like a combination of arm, hand, and fingers.

© STEVE BLOOM IMAGES/ALAMY (INSET); © FOUR OAKS/SHUTTERSTOCK.COM (HERD)

2

Do Elephants TALK?

Earth's largest land animals have a lot to say—even when they don't seem to be making a sound.

TEXT BY PETER WINKLER

Translating infrasound helps scientists begin to understand elephant behavior. For example, it turns out that the elephants heading to the water hole may have heard warning calls from another herd. Perhaps a lion was slurping water and looking hungry. The cat would be no match for an adult elephant, but it might kill a calf. No drink would be worth that risk, so the herd turned away.

▲ Trouble Ahead?
Lions sometimes attack elephant calves, so this elephant might warn herds to stay away.

Big Eater.
An adult can scarf down 300 pounds of leaves and grass in just one day.

LONG-DISTANCE CALLS

Elephants use infrasound to communicate many types of messages over long distances. Some of their talk helps hold families together. To understand how this works, you need to know a little about elephant families.

Females spend their lives with mothers, sisters, and children. They form tight-knit herds of 10 to 20 members. The oldest female elephant—the **matriarch**—takes charge. Males live with a herd until they are teens. Then they depart. They live alone or join with other males in a "bachelor herd."

The members of a herd often scatter over large areas to seek food for their mighty appetites. (An adult elephant can eat 300 pounds of grass and plants in a single day!) Long-distance calls let elephants know where their relatives are. And when the matriarch says, "Come here!" the herd gathers within minutes.

Like curious kittens, elephant calves sometimes wander off and get into trouble. When that happens, they cry for help. Adults respond with infrasound calls and other noises: "It's okay. We're coming to help you."

Adult males and females often live far apart, so they use infrasound to find each other at mating time. Females mate only once every four years or so. When a female is ready, she makes a special series of calls. Males who hear the calls storm toward her. Sometimes two or more males battle fiercely for a chance to court the female.

© GERRIT_DE_VRIES/SHUTTERSTOCK.COM

WWF—Elephant Style.
Playful and social, young elephants make a pair of Wild Wrestling Friends. Their muddy coats block heat and flies.

HEARING AIDS

Elephants tune in to all this talk with their large, powerful ears. An African elephant's ears can grow to be six feet long and four feet wide. (Asian elephants have much smaller ears.) When straining to hear something, the animal turns toward the sound and opens its ears wide.

At the same time, the elephant may raise its trunk to sniff at the wind. Elephants have a keen sense of smell. Odors may help them figure out what they're hearing.

Elephants may have yet another way of learning what's going on around them. Although scientists haven't proved it, some scientists think elephants can feel infrasound as the sound waves travel through the ground.

DISTRESS CALL

Communication skills help Earth's largest land animals survive in the wild. But even these skills can't save elephants from **extinction.**

In 1997 Africa's elephant population was about 500,000. That may seem like a lot, but there were 1.3 million African elephants in 1979. More than half of the elephant population vanished in only 18 years.

How did this happen? **Poachers** killed many elephants for their ivory tusks, because ivory can be sold for a lot of money.

And a growing human population wiped out vast amounts of elephant **habitat** to build farms and towns. Elephants from these areas wandered into human settlements. Some elephants ate valuable crops and made some farmers angry enough to kill them.

HOW WILL WE ANSWER?

Conservationists are working hard to save elephants. Wildlife groups are trying to persuade people around the world to stop buying ivory.

Elephant supporters are also working with African communities to maintain parks where elephants can be safe and will not harm crops. Some conservationists hope that tourists will visit these beloved animals there. That would mean jobs for local people, who would then view elephants as a resource to protect.

WORDWise ✕✕✕✕✕

calf: the young of some large animals, such as whales and elephants (plural: *calves*)

conservationist: a person who protects natural resources

extinction: the end of an entire species

habitat: the place where something lives

herd: a group of one type of animal that stays together

infrasound: sound so low that humans can't hear it

matriarch: a female who leads a herd

pitch: how high or low a sound is

poacher: one who kills or takes wild animals illegally

spectrograph: a machine that translates recorded sound waves into images

Super

size

Really Tall
Really Tough
Really Big

Elephants are big. In fact, they're the largest animals that live on land. They can reach a height of ten feet. They're heavy too. They can weigh up to 12,000 pounds, or six tons.

It's no surprise that elephants have big features too. Those big ears, trunk, and tusks aren't just for show. Such supersize features actually help an elephant survive.

BIG EARS

Elephants rely on all their senses. They use their hearing, sight, smell, touch, and taste. Hearing is especially important. That's because their eyesight isn't all that good.

Big ears help an elephant know when danger is near. They pick up tiny noises that mean terrible trouble. For instance, they hear the rustling of a hungry lion in tall grass.

Big ears also help elephants keep track of one another. They can hear elephant calls even from far away.

You might never guess that big ears also help an elephant keep cool. How? In hot weather, they act like giant fans. With the twitch of an ear, an elephant can stir up its own little breeze.

A NEAT NOSE

Ears aren't an elephant's only cool feature. Its trunk is neat too. Elephants use their trunks for just about everything they do.

Elephants use their trunks to sniff the air for danger. They also use their trunks to eat, drink, bathe, scratch an itch, lift heavy objects, and talk to other elephants. Imagine having a nose that did all that!

An elephant's trunk has thousands of muscles. It is strong enough to lift fallen trees. But the trunk is also very sensitive. An elephant can pick up a peanut with the tip of its trunk—and shell it too.

TOUGH TEETH

Elephants need some seriously tough teeth. Some of these teeth are for chewing. Others—the tusks—have a much different use.

You see, tusks are more than just teeth. They're all-in-one tools. Elephants dig in the ground with their tusks. With their tusks, they strip bark off trees for a tasty snack. Tusks are perfect for uprooting small bushes and trees too.

Along with the other supersize features, tusks help elephants survive in the wild.

Big Beasts.
Elephants are the planet's largest land animals. Their huge features help these big beasts survive.

Ecosystems
and Elephants

E lephants are large—and so is their impact on the ecosystem. An ecosystem includes the plants and animals that live nearby, as well as the air, water, and soil. Elephants are big enough that they actually shape their ecosystem.

BIG ANIMALS WITH BIG ROLES

Did you know that elephants can change the shape of the land! How do they do it? Just by walking and eating.

Imagine you're in a grassland. Look! A herd of elephants is trudging by. They're on their way to a watering hole. There are many elephants. Their feet wear paths in the grass.

Elephants have big appetites. So as they walk, they pause to tear up mouthfuls of grass. Sometimes they knock over young trees. They munch on the twigs, leaves, and roots.

This might sound destructive. But without elephants, the grassland would soon be overrun by trees. So elephants help grasslands stay healthy and strong.

HEALTHY FORESTS TOO

Some elephants live in forests. They help keep forests healthy too. They create trails through the brush. They make clearings in the woods.

See the elephant scraping bark off a tree with its tusks? This tree will die without its bark. When it falls, a small clearing will form. Sunlight will shine through. Young trees will begin to grow. Smaller animals will find new homes.

This is part of keeping the forest strong. It's one way that elephants help the world.

Changing the Land.
Elephants are big beasts. They have a big impact on the places where they live.

Grassland Giants.
Elephants have a role in keeping grasslands healthy.

Clearing the Way.
An elephant uses its tusks to create a clearing in the forest.

ELEPHANTS IN AFRICA

ASIA

EUROPE

AFRICA

ATLANTIC OCEAN

Nile River

Nile River

Congo River

Niger River

ATLAS MOUNTAINS

S A H A R A

Most of Africa is made up of high, flat land. There are few mountains. Deserts cover the northern and southern tips of the continent. Rain forests grow along the Equator. Grasslands called savannas fill most of the remaining land.

Elephant Population

We are not sure how many elephants live in Africa. It is hard for humans to trudge through thick wilderness to find the animals. The counts we have are good guesses, or estimates. These estimates include the number of elephants that people have spotted from the ground and the air. Some estimated numbers also come from elephant tracks and other clues.

Questions

1. Look at the map. In what land regions do most African elephants live?

2. Look at the population chart below. In which area of Africa are population counts the least definite? Why do you think that is?

Area	Definitely This Many	Probably This Many More	Possibly This Many More Still
Central Africa	7,320	81,657	128,648
Eastern Africa	90,292	16,707	20,190
Southern Africa	170,120	16,382	34,660
Western Africa	2,771	1,232	5,024

Source: International Union for Conservation of Nature and Natural Resources/African Elephant Specialist Group, 1997

Map Key

- Mountains
- Rain Forest
- Grassland (Savanna)
- Desert
- Wetland
- Areas Where Many Elephants Live

INDIAN OCEAN

MADAGASCAR

Lake Victoria

Lake Tanganyika

Lake Malawi

Great Rift

Zambezi River

KALAHARI DESERT

DRAKENSBERG

N E S W

MAP/MARTIN WALZ
ILLUSTRATION/STUART ARMSTRONG

Elephants

Answer these questions to find out what you learned about elephants.

1 What kinds of things might elephants say to each other?

2 What parts of an elephant help it survive in its environment?

3 In what ways are elephants threatened by people?

4 What elephant activities could cause problems for farmers?

5 If elephants became extinct, how would their ecosystem change?